Where Are
My
Susannas?

Where Are My Susannas?

Susan Hyatt

with a conclusion by

Barbara Silver

Hyatt Int'l Ministrsies, Inc.
P. O. Box 700276
Tulsa, OK 74170
1997

Published by Hyatt International Ministries, Inc.
P. O. Box 78, Chicota, Texas 75425
P. O. Box 700276, Tulsa, OK 74170

Cover and book design by Susan Hyatt

All Scripture References are taken from
the New International and the New King James Versions
of the Bible unless otherwise stated.

91 92 93 94 95 96 10 9 8 7 6 5 4 3 2 1

ISBN 1-888435-03-8
Printed in the United States of America

Contents

Chapter 1

Was That You, God?

O NE SUNDAY EVENING in the summer of 1991, my husband Eddie was preaching in a small country church in Canada. He and four other men were seated in the place of honor on the platform, and I was seated in the congregation. Early in the service as we worshipped the Lord, a question flooded my mind: *Where are My Susannas?* What an interesting question! It came without warning, and it completely captured my attention.

I opened my eyes and looked around. There were no *Susannas* on the platform. In the congregation there were a couple of men and several women.

In a flash, a second question flooded my mind: *Where are My Phoebes?* And as quickly and unexpectantly, a third question came: *Where are My Aimees?*

I knew *Susanna* was a reference to Susanna Wesley, the mother of John Wesley. I knew too that *Phoebe* referred to Phoebe Palmer, pivotal figure in the nineteenth century Holiness Movement, and Aimee, to Aimee Semple McPherson, the famous Pentecostal preacher of this century.

I also knew instinctively that the Lord was talking to me. He had called each one of these women by her first name and had prefaced each reference with the pronoun *My*. *My* Susannas, *My* Phoebes, and *My* Aimees. In addition, each one was in the plural: Susannas, Phoebes, and Aimees. Obviously, He was referring to these women as types, as examples, as models.

Furthermore, the Spirit of the Lord had posed questions. This technique has normally been God's way of getting my attention and focusing my thinking to tell me something important. So quickly, I recollected a few facts about Susanna, about Phoebe, and about Aimee.

Later in the service, when I was invited to address the congregation, I posed the same three questions and sketched some details of the lives of these three women. Although the immediate impact on the congregation may have been minimal, I knew I had had an encounter with the Lord. The impact of that encounter lingers. The questions still challenge me.

Chapter 2

Where Are
My Susannas?

S USANNA ANNESLEY WESLEY (1669-1742) lived in England at a time when formal education was neither a privilege nor a right enjoyed by women. Despite this, she grew to be a learned and liberated[1] woman with a strong sense both of personal worth and personal responsibility. She refused to yield to the hardships of poverty. She would not succumb to the constraints of culture. She would not surrender to religious restrictions of gender-biased religion. She would find a way to overcome, to bring change, and to obey God. And she made an impact in her day, the fruit of which continues to our day.

---

[1] Frank Baker, "Susanna Wesley: Puritan, Parent, Pastor, Protagonist, Pattern," *Women in New Worlds* (Nashville: Abingdon, 1982), 113.

Where Are My Susannas?

Susanna was the youngest of twenty-five Annesley siblings. Her father, an English Puritan known as the *Saint Paul of Nonconformity,* seemed to take special interest in her, educating her "in solid piety." He included her in frequent discussions with his well-educated, theological colleagues.[2] Impressed by this intellectual and spiritual climate, while still in her teens, Susanna taught herself Hebrew, Greek, and Latin in order to study the Bible and early Christian literature in the original languages. This equipped her to search the Scriptures and to grapple personally with the many issues raised in the theological arena of her day.

Susanna married Samuel Wesley, an Anglican priest. Of their nineteen children, only seven reached adulthood. Quite a remarkable mother, she considered parental responsibility a divine mandate. In a letter to her son John, she reflected on this, saying,

> There's few (if any) that would entirely devote above twenty years of the prime of life in hope to save the souls of their children (which they think may be saved without much ado); for

---

[2] John Wesley Chilcote, *John Wesley and the Women Preachers of Early Methodism* (Metuchen, NJ: Scarecrow, 1991), 17; Frank Baker, "Salute to Susanna," *Methodist History* 7 (April 1969): 3-12; John Haggai, "Women in the Lead," *Charisma*, Nov. 1987, 25-32.

that was my principle intention, however un-skillfully and unsuccessfully managed.[3]

Because Susanna believed that God had uniquely gifted each child, she nurtured each one with puprpose. One method she used was to spend an hour each week alone with each child. As she interacted with each one during this time, she discerned and developed those precious talents.

In son Charles (1707-1788), for example, she noticed a special aptitude for words, rhythm, and music. So she provided activities and encouragement to cultivate this dominant feature of his personality. It wasn't by chance or accident, then, that Charles became the great hymn writer of the Wesleyan Revival. It was by divine design and human cooperation! The result? The Church still enjoys his magnificent hymns.[4] Consider the ageless beauty of just this one:

O for a thousand tongues to sing
My dear Redeemer's praise,

---

[3] Chilcote, 18.

[4] *The Methodist Hymnal.* Nashville: The Methodist Book Concern, 1939. See Hymn numbers 25, 32, 84, 137, 154, 155, 162, 169, 171, 183, 186, 189, 191, 200-203, 208, 211, 217-18, 229, 282, 287, 290, 299, 309, 311, 338, 339, 343, 356, 370, 371, 372, 373, 377, 400, 402, 403, 404, 417, 419, 422, 444, 500, 518, 522, 536, 538, 540.

Where Are My Susannas?

The glories of my God and King,
The triumphs of His grace!

My gracious Master and my God,
Assist me to proclaim,
To spread through all the earth abroad
The honors of Thy name.

Jesus! the name that charms our fears,
That bids our sorrows cease,
'Tis music in the sinner's ears,
'Tis life and health and peace.

He breaks the power of cancelled sin,
He sets the prisoner free;
His blood can make the foulest clean,
His blood availed for me.

He speaks, and, listening to His voice,
New life the dead receive,
The mournful broken heart's rejoice,
The humble poor believe.

Hear Him, ye deaf; His praise, ye dumb,
Your loosened tongues employ;
Ye blind, behold your Saviour come;
And leap, ye lame, for joy.

See all your sins on Jesus laid:
   The Lamb of God was slain;
His soul was once an offering made
   For every soul of man.

Glory to God, and praise, and love
   Be ever, ever given
By saints below and saints above,
   The Church in earth and heaven.

Son John (1703-1791), she observed, had an unusual sense of destiny and was especially enthusiastic about the Bible. So she coached him to proficiency in Hebrew and Greek and required extensive memorization of Scripture. She writes,

[I determined] to be more particularly careful of the soul of this child that thou hast so mercifully provided for, than ever I have been, that I may do my endeavour to instill into his mind ţhe principles of the true religion and virtue.

In this manner, then, Susanna's pastoral gifts were developed first at home. Then they found expression in public. This happened when her husband, Rev. Samuel Wesley, was thrown into

---

[5] Chilcote, 20.

debtor's prison. In his absence, a curate filled the parish pulpit. Susanna and the children continued to live in the Epworth rectory, where, on Sunday evenings, she conducted family devotions. Everyone was welcome, and soon crowds of 300 were jamming into the residence. At the same time, Evensong, conducted by the curate in the sanctuary, drew only twenty-five or thirty people.

Riled by the enthusiastic response to Susanna's family devotions, the curate charged her with "conducting a clandestine conventicle and usurping the authority of her husband."[6] When Samuel confronted her with the curate's charges, she boldly defended her right to continue the meetings. She pointed to both the numerical and spiritual success of her endeavors. She appealed as well to the positive social effect of her ministry, noting the "improved relationships among the townspeople and increased fervor and desire for the things of God."[7] She argued,

> If you do, after all, think fit to dissolve this assembly, do not tell me that you desire me to do it, for that will not satisfy my conscience: but send me your positive command, in such full and express terms as may absolve me from

---

[6] Chilcote, 20.

[7] Chilcote, 20.

all guilt and punishment for neglecting this opportunity of doing good when you and I shall appear before the great and awful tribunal of our Lord Jesus Christ.[8]

Samuel responded by supporting Susanna. The evidence in her favor was overwhelming indeed, and her bold insistence was obviously not motivated by misguided self-importance or stiff-necked rebellion. In defiance of cultural restrictions based on gender, she continued to minister and the parish flourished in her husband's absence. Without the titles, regalia, training, liturgy, or sanction of the State church, Susanna got the job done! Despite her lack of formal education, she exhibited superior theological skills and biblical knowledge as well as effective leadership skills and pastoral ability.

In accomplishing this, Susanna Wesley did an amazing thing. While remaining loyal to the Anglican Church, at least politically, she was in fact practicing the theological persuasions of the Nonconformists among whom she developed her own informed theology. For all practical purposes, she ignored the mediatoral position maintained by the Anglican church and the Anglican priesthood. She opted, in practice, for "the sanctity of the inner conscience and the present activity of the Holy

---

[8] Chilcote, 20.

Spirit"[9] in the life of the believer. In other words, she believed it was her personal responsibility to obey, first and foremost, the Holy Spirit when this proved contrary to the dictates of the State church.

This determination to obey the Holy Spirit was grounded in Biblical literacy, theological reflection, and personal experience. It produced in her a dependence on God that permitted a healthy detachment from the need for human approval and hence from the control of human opinion. Evidence of this appears in her writings. For example, in a letter to Lady Yarborough written in 1702, Susanna says,

> I value neither reputation, friends, or anything, in comparison of the simple satisfaction of preserving a conscience void of offense towards God and man.[10]

This position, coupled with a God-directed sense of responsibility and caring for people, made Susanna a remarkable person indeed. In a letter to her husband during his stint in prison, she writes, "I cannot but look upon every soul you leave under my care as a talent committed to me under a trust by the great Lord of all the families."[11] This statement highlights Susanna's integrity. That is to say,

---

[9] Chilcote, 19.

[10] Chilcote, 19.

[11] Chilcote, 19.

the Susanna who nurtured her children was the same Susanna who nurtured the people of the parish. She seemed to see each person as a special trust from God. In each one, she sought that unique gifting divinely deposited by the Creator God for His service and glory. Whereas in the State church, ritual provided the construct for righteous religious behavior, for Susanna, relationship with God and with others constituted true piety.

Given the restrictions of her day, Susanna Wesley achieved remarkable woman. Her influence never really died. She has been regarded by some as the pivotal figure who facilitated the eighteenth-century Methodist Revival that saved England from the ravages of a bloody revolution. This revival also spawned the great nineteenth-century Methodist-Holiness Revival in America that was the forerunner of the explosive Pentecostal/Charismatic Revival of the twentieth century.

Traditional history regards Susanna's son, John Wesley, as the *Father of Methodism.* However, for various legitimate reasons, Susanna, may indeed be considered its founder. Her perceptive, conscientious guidance during her son's formative years equipped him with Biblical tools, theological perspectives, and a holy lifestyle that enabled him to turn a nation from sin to salvation, from near-revolution to rest, from fragmentation to focus, and from instability to solidarity. In addition, the

11

power of example should never be underestimated! Susanna's family devotions served as pattern for the Methodist societies he instituted as cells to nurture spiritual life within the existing structure. Furthermore, as a result of his mother's counsel and example as a teacher, Wesley began appointing women as class leaders in 1739, and between 1761 and 1791 he appointed women as local preachers and itinerant ministers. Furthermore, throughout her life, Susanna was, in fact, her son's most trusted and most influential counselor.

Various researchers have recognized Susanna's importance in Methodism. For example, John Chilcote, in his 1991 work, *John Wesley and the Women Preachers of Early Methodism*, writes,

> In her style of life, spiritual and intellectual disciplines, theological acumen, and ecclesiastical sensibility she was set forward as the paradigm[12] of the Methodist woman for years to come.

Wesleyan scholar, Frank Baker, notes in his article, "Susanna Wesley, Apologist for Methodism," that Susanna was Methodism's instigator, initial theologian, and apologist.[13] Significant literature of the

---

[12] Chilcote, 18.

[13] Frank Baker, "Susanna Wesley, Apologist for Methodism," Wesley Historical Society 35 (Sept. 1965): 68-71.

nineteenth century Holiness Movement concurs, and Benjamin St. James Fry, writing in 1892, remarks,

> If I were asked to name the beginning of the present revival of the spirit and practice of the first century . . . I should name Susanna Wesley . . . persisting in her conviction of duty against the advice of rector and curate, prompted no doubt, by the Holy Spirit.[14]

Also writing in 1892, Charles Wesley Rishell notes, "From the beginning Methodism has granted to women a large liberty in public dress, beginning with Susanna Wesley."[15]

Susanna was also highly acclaimed by women of the Holiness Movement. Mrs. Jennie Fowler Willing, an editor of the prestigious Holiness periodical, *The Guide to Holiness*, spoke highly of her. In an 1898 article, she said that Susanna was, "the founder of a religious organization that . . . girdled the globe with a grand gospel of salvation from sin, a holy inspiration to millions of souls."[16]

---

[14] Benjamin St. James Fry, *Woman's Work in the Church* (New York: Hunt and Eaton, 1892), 1.

[15] Charles Wesley Rishell, *The Official Recognition of Woman in the Church* (New York: Hunt and Eaton, 1892), 62-63.

[16] Mrs. Jennie Willing Flower, "Woman Under the Pentecostal Baptism," *The Guide to Holiness* 69 (Sept. 1892): 84.

Where Are My Susannas?

WHAT WAS IT ABOUT SUSANNA THAT PROMPTED THE LORD TO POSE THE QUESTION, "WHERE ARE MY SUSANNAS?"

Was it her sense of responsibility to nurture faithfully and with divine sensitivity those entrusted to her care? Was it her persistence in remaining true to God despite the disgrace of an incarcerated husband and the awful hardship of poverty? Was it her motivation to know the Scriptures, so much so that she learned languages that are today reserved primarily for seminary students? Was it her determination to do what she knew in her heart was right despite hostile cultural views, gender-biased religion, and disparaging opinion?

"Where are My Susannas?" the Lord asks.

Chapter 3

Where Are
My Phoebes?

P HOEBE WORRALL PALMER (1807-1874)[1]
grew up in a devout Methodist home in New
York City. Early in life, she made a whole-
hearted commitment to serve the Lord. She was
consumed with a hunger to know Him.

Phoebe married Dr. Walter Clarke Palmer
(1804-1883),[2] a prominent New York physician.
Like Phoebe, he too had a passion to serve the Lord
and decided that the most effective means of his

---

[1] Dayton and Dayton, "Women in the Holiness Movement,"
Photocopy, n.d., 5; Harold E. Raser, *Phoebe Palmer: Her Life
and Thought* (Lewiston, NY: Edwin Mellen Press, 1987);
Charles Edward White, "Phoebe Palmer and the Development
of Pentecostal Pneumatology," *Wesleyan Theological Journal* (12
June 1990): 208.

[2] Raser, 30ff.

doing so would be to become a medical doctor. So Dr. and Mrs. Palmer served faithfully as members of the affluent Methodist Church in New York City.

As children came along, Phoebe became a doting mother. Totally consumed with parenting, the time she once gave to the Lord, she now gave to her children. What a devastating blow it was then, when her first two babies died in tragic accidents in her loving home. Filled with unbearable grief, Phoebe found herself on her knees, desperate for the answer to that nagging question, "Why?"

The answer she heard was this: *She had devoted herself to her children to such an extent that these gifts from God had actually displaced God in her life. They had become idols!*

Immediately she repented. For Phoebe, this meant turning from a life ruled by temporal concerns to a life directed by eternal values. With this established, Phoebe soon gave birth to two more precious children. This time, Mother Phoebe kept her purpose and priorities lined up with God's will. This alignment meant, among other things, sharing with nannies the care of her children. God blessed this decision and her offspring henceforth enjoyed long and prosperous lives. Perhaps it could be said that when Phoebe looked after God's business, God looked after her business!

Obedience to the call resulted in Phoebe becoming one of the most influential Christian leaders of the 1800s. She has, in fact, been recognized as the "major force behind a mid-nineteenth century reaffirmation of the Wesleyan doctrine of Christian perfection" that spawned a major revival.[3] Known as the Holiness Movement, this revival ignited flames first among the Methodists as they sought to recover the religious fervor of the Wesleyan Revival of the previous century. In an effort to rekindle Methodism's original fire, the Methodist Conferences of 1824 and 1832 had called the faithful to return to holy living. John Wesley's teaching on sanctification as a second work of grace in the life of the believer came to the forefront again. This pursuit of holiness was based on Hebrews 12:14, which states, *Pursue peace with all, and holiness (sanctification), without which no one will see the Lord.*

As Phoebe sought this second blessing, she struggled with the emphasis placed on feeling as evidence of having received the experience. As hard as she tried, she just could not achieve that *feeling.* Finally, she saw that she could—in fact, must—

---

[3] Dayton, "Evangelical Roots," 13; Synan, Lectures (1991); M. Simpson, "Drew Seminary and Female College," and "Drew Theological Seminary," *Cyclopedia of Methodism* (Philadelphia: Louis Everts, 1881), 312;. Melvin Dieter, *The Holiness Revival of the Nineteenth Century* (Metuchen: Scarecrow, 1980), 26.

accept it by "naked faith in the naked Word."[4] She read, *For which is greater, the gift or the altar that sanctifies the gift? (Mt. 23:19)*. She understood in a new way that the altar was the place of total surrender to God where the shed blood of the Lord Jesus provided both salvation and cleansing. In obedience to Romans 12:1, she presented herself a living sacrifice on the altar and by faith received sanctification as an accomplished fact. If she needed experiential evidence, it came in the form of a new dimension of peace. It was July 26, 1837.

Phoebe Phoebe also understood the Biblical principle of confessing what she had received by faith. She had gained this understanding from the writings of Wesley's theological colleague, John Fletcher. She writes,

> One must confess the blessing on the basis of faith alone (Rom. 10:9-10). Do not forget that believing with the heart and confessing with the mouth stand closely connected. What God hath joined together let not man put asunder.[5]

Phoebe's revolutionary approach to sanctification rapidly gained recognition among the Methodists. Before long it exerted influence among the

---

[4] Raser, 47.

[5] Raser, 175.

non-Wesleyan denominations as well. This *altar terminology* and *shorter way* to sanctification became standards in the revival.

So powerful was the revival that it spread to every denomination in America and spanned the Atlantic to the British Isles. Non-Wesleyans usually preferred non-Wesleyan terminology to describe their new dimension of Christian experience. Presbyterians called it the *higher Christian life*, and Baptists spoke of it as *the rest of faith*. Eventually, most denominations adopted Pentecostal terminology referring to the experience as *the baptism in the Holy Spirit*. Phoebe Palmer, more than any other person, was responsible for this shift in terminology.

Ultimately, and very much to Phoebe's credit, Pentecostal language replaced Wesleyan terminology in describing *the second blessing*. Instead of *sanctification* it became *the baptism of the Holy Ghost;* and instead of *cleansing from sin,* the blessing consisted of *an endowment of power.* These trends were important developments as the church moved toward the twentieth century and the explosion of the modern Pentecostal/Charismatic movement.

It soon becomes obvious that Phoebe was a pivotal figure in the Holiness Movement. She was, in fact, its dominant theologian, a foremost Bible teacher, a prominent evangelist, and perhaps its most influential writer and editor. This influence can be traced to 1840 when she became the leader

of the *Tuesday Meeting for the Promotion of Holiness.*
This meeting was conducted in the Palmer's spa-
cious parlor and drew many prominent churchmen
from both within and without the Methodism.
Among those sanctified in her parlor were four
leading Methodist bishops. Travelers to New York
City were welcome visitors to the *Tuesday Meeting.*

For twenty years, beginning in 1841, the call to
minister kept Phoebe away from home most of the
time. During this period, Dr. Palmer presided over
the home and vigorously supported his wife's ministry in every possible way. He cheerfully financed
her travels, since she often ministered without re-
ceiving an honorarium. In addition, he went into
the publishing business to increase Phoebe's reach
as an author,[6] and eventually he closed his medical
practice and accompanied Phoebe in ministry.[7]

Although Phoebe was in ministry full-time, she
confesses to being "a reluctant preacher." Neverthe-
less, as she obeyed the Lord, she found herself
"pioneering alone in a man's world."[8] She did not
pursue official church ordination. The fruit of her
ministry stands alone as a testimony to the Divine
Source and integrity of her call. At least 25,000

---

[6] Raser, 106-107.

[7] Raser, 63.

[8] Phoebe Palmer, *The Way of Holiness* (New York: W. C.
Palmer, 1843, 1867), 37-38.

people in the Northeastern United States, in Eastern Canada, and in England were converted during her meetings that ran from a few days to several weeks. In addition, countless hundreds were sanctified, or *baptized in the Spirit,* as she called it.

In her book, *Four Years in the Old World,* Phoebe records the events of an extended time of ministry that she and her husband spent in England. Describing her meetings in the City of Newcastle, Phoebe says, "The Lord was saving the people by scores daily."[9] At the time of the report, the names of over 2000 people were already on record as having received the blessing "of pardon or purity." God was moving through her ministry in such a powerful manner that she remarks, "Now the entire community seems ready to acknowledge its [the revival's] power."[10] She notes, "The power of God is sensibly felt to be present to heal."[11] She speaks of those who "felt the girdings of almighty power in an unusual manner," and of the "tokens of divine presence."[12] Phoebe regarded the mighty manifestations of the Spirit as evidence of "a resuscitation of

---

[9] Phoebe Palmer, *Four Years in the Old World* (Boston: Foster & Palmer, 1865), 145.

[10] Palmer, 145.

[11] Palmer, 103.

[12] Palmer, 111.

primitive Christianity and primitive Methodism."[13]

The manifestations of the Spirit in the Newcastle meetings were by no means isolated incidents. Revival-type manifestations were typical in her meetings. Writing from Sunderland, England, she says that there was such a sense of the divine presence that "people are weeping all over the house."[14]

In addition to being a mightily anointed Bible teacher and revivalist, Phoebe gained considerable recognition as a theologian. Charles Edward White, in his scholarly article, "Phoebe Palmer and the Development of Pentecostal Pneumatology," published in the *Wesleyan Theological Journal* in 1990, calls Phoebe "the most influential female theologian the Church has yet produced."[15] Harold E. Raser, in his thorough study, *Phoebe Palmer: Her Life and Thought* published three years earlier in 1987, had already concluded that Phoebe Palmer, as a theologian, had given the Holiness Movement concrete identity and theological focus.[16]

In the early days of her ministry, Phoebe used Wesleyan terminology such as *sanctification* and *cleansing* when referring to *the second blessing*. How-

---

[13] Palmer, 107.

[14] Palmer, 120.

[15] White, 208.

[16] Raser, 199.

ever, she shifted to what has been called *Pentecostal terminology* in discussing the second blessing.[17] For example, writing from England, she says that the emphasis of the afternoon meetings is "the full baptism of the Holy Spirit, as received by the one hundred and twenty disciples on the day of Pentecost."[18]

This Spirit baptism affected a person's speech in the same manner that outpouring of the Holy Spirit had affected the speech of the hundred and twenty in the Upper Room (Acts 2:4). In describing this occurrence at one of her meetings, Phoebe says, "The baptism of fire descended; and, as in the early days of Christianity, utterance as a restraining gift was also given."[19] On another occasion, a local preacher was the first to receive this "tongue of fire," and according to Phoebe, he "spake as the Spirit gave utterance."[20]

Despite the fruitfulness of her ministry, Phoebe endured considerable rejection and criticism because she was a woman functioning in public ministry. Perhaps her most vocal critic was Hiram Matti-

---

[17] Donald Dayton, "Christian Perfection to the Baptism of the Holy Ghost," *Aspects of Pentecostal-Charismatic Origins*, Vinson Synan Ed. (Plainfield: Logos, 1975), 39-54.

[18] Palmer, *Four Years in the Old World*, 107.

[19] Palmer, 127.

[20] Palmer, 96.

son. In *The Christian Advocate and Journal* (29 Nov. 1855), he writes, "Are we so ignorant [of holiness] as to require a <u>sister</u> to travel from conference to conference to instruct us?"[21] Likewise, reacting to Phoebe and in particular, to her first book, *The Way of Holiness,* another male critic suggested Palmer would have "been better engaged in washing dishes than in writing."[22]

Prompted by criticism of this sort and by recognition of the need for a clearly articulated Biblical theology for the right of women to minister publicly, Phoebe wrote *The Promise of the Father.* Published in 1859, this 421-page book is a theological treatise validating women's right and responsibility to obey the call to public ministry.[23] She proposed a three-pronged Biblical argument.

- The first line of argument is based on **salvation.** Paul encapsulates this position in Galatians 3:26-29. This verse, Phoebe asserted, eliminates unequivocally any restrictions based on gender.

  [26]You are all children of God through faith in Christ Jesus, [27]for all of you who were baptized

---

[21] Hiram Mattison, *The Christian Advocate and Journal* (29 Nov. 1855): 189.

[22] Raser, 365.

[23] Phoebe Palmer, *The Promise of the Father,* or *A Neglected Specialty of the Last Days* (Boston: Henry V. Degen, 1859).

*into Christ have clothed yourselves with Christ.
[28]There is neither Jew nor Greek, slave nor free,
there is neither male nor female, for you are all one
in Christ Jesus. [29]If you belong to Christ, then you
are Abraham's seed, and heirs according to the
promise (Gal. 3:26-29 NIV - Inclusive Language Ed. 1995).*

- The second line of argument is based on **sanctification**. In Phoebe's theology of holiness, based on Hebrews 12:14, every believer was to receive by faith this cleansing and empowering experience subsequent to salvation. Then according to Romans 10:9-10, each believer was to testify to having received it. This Biblical mandate, in particular, over-ruled the prevailing law of female silence. Women as well as men were to testify publicly!

- The third line of argument was the **Pentecostal** argument. This appealed to the event prophesied in Joel 2:28 and reported in Acts 2:17-18.

*And it shall come to pass in the last days, says
God, That I will pour out My Spirit on all flesh;
Your sons and your daughters shall prophesy,
Your young men shall see visions, Your old men
shall dream dreams. And also on My menservants
and on My maidservants I will pour out My
Spirit in those days; And they shall prophesy
(Acts 2:17-18).*

Where Are My Susannas?

This Pentecostal argument was eschatological, that is, it had to do with prophesied events concerning the End-Times. It focused on the significance of the outpouring of the Holy Spirit in the last days and the fact that men and women were equal recipients of this outpouring. Furthermore, this outpouring was perceived as empowerment for ministry. The *gift of power* to prophesy, that is, *to herald the glad tidings to every creature* was given equally to men and women alike on the Day of Pentecost. Phoebe therefore asserts that equal right to speak and minister was to be a present reality among believers.[24]

Phoebe concludes her argument saying, "It is the intention of God that women, whom he has equipped to minister in his Church, be given the right to express their spiritual gifts."[25] She asserts, therefore, that both men and women would be "expected and compelled to pray, prophesy and preach."[26] She reasons,

> [On the Day of Pentecost] did one of that
> waiting company wait in vain; or did the clo-
> ven tongue of fire appear to all, and sit upon

---

[24] Raser, 202; Palmer, 14, 23.

[25] Raser, 199-210.

[26] Dayton and Dayton, 6; Richard Wheatley, *The Life and Letters of Mrs. Phoebe Palmer* (New York: Palmer and Hughes, 1876), 496-497.

"each" waiting disciple, irrespective of sex? Surely, this was that spoken by the prophet Joel; and thus has the Holy Spirit expressly declared through Peter [referring to the account of Pentecost, Acts 2]. . . . The dispensation of the Spirit was now entered upon,— the last dispensation previous to the last glorious appearing of our Lord and Saviour Jesus Christ. The Spirit now descended alike on all. And they were all filled with the Holy Ghost, and began to speak as the Spirit gave utterance.[27]

Phoebe seems to have limited her revolutionary proposals concerning women's right to speak and be heard respectfully to church meetings. She sidesteps the issue of equal privilege and responsibility in the domestic and civil arenas. In these she appears to have maintained the traditional view of role based on gender with women being subordinate to men. According to Phoebe, women are to be "domestic overseers" because "woman's sphere" is the home and family, and are to be "subordinate religious foot soldiers who should function through various voluntary religious associations."[28]

---

[27] Wheatley, 496-497.

[28] Raser, 367.

Phoebe precludes this view, however, when she acknowledges that the demands of "Spirit baptized religious activism" could take a "woman largely out of the home." In fact, she acknowledges that a woman "seeking entire sanctification" might have to give up to God her spouse and family "attachments which may distract her from 'religious duties' God may require."[29]

Essentially, Phoebe's major concern was not change "in the social or domestic relations."[30] Instead she promoted the idea of men and women together in partnership, entirely consecrated to God, empowered through the baptism of the Holy Ghost, and free to preach the Gospel.[31] One cannot help but wonder if the apparent limits of her proposal were due, at least in part, to her own favorable domestic and marital circumstances! A woman of considerable intelligence and of elite New York City social status, she enjoyed the support of her husband in every respect.

Regardless, Phoebe's position on women's status was progressive, if not revolutionary. She indeed argues toward a position of Biblical equality. Harold Raser, in *Phoebe Palmer: Her Life and Thought*

---

[29] Raser, 367; Wheatly, 597-598.

[30] Raser, 210.

[31] Raser, 210.

says that she instigated "a self-conscious female community of religious activism, which provided identity outside the home and a political training ground."[32] In addition, he says that she contributed

> to an expanded role for women first in the church and the eventual opening up of the very social issues Palmer herself skirted. This in turn strengthened the hand of women seeking feminine equality in the larger society.[33]

According to Holiness scholar, Donald Dayton, *The Promise of the Father* was "the fountainhead of innumerable feminist arguments developed through the remainder of the nineteenth century and into the twentieth."[34]

Phoebe's anointed ministry—her preaching, teaching, and theological writings—had wide-ranging and significant influence. Besides individual lives that were changed through her preaching, thousands who never met her were influenced by her impact as editor of the major Holiness periodical *The Guide to Holiness* (1864-1874). Moreover, she was a founder of prestigious Drew University (1866/1868) in Madison, New Jersey. In addition,

---

[32] Raser, 367.

[33] Raser, 210.

[34] Donald Dayton, *Discovering an Evangelical History* (New York: Harper and Row, 1976), 96.

her dynamic example inspired giants of the faith such as Catherine Booth and Amanda Smith.[35]

Catherine Mumford Booth (1829-1890), who "laid the first stone of the Salvation Army"[36] worked tirelessly for equal authority, equal rights, and equal responsibilities for women on the basis of redemption and Pentecost.[37] In the marriage relationship, she staunchly refused to be considered or treated anything but equal with her husband, William Booth (1829-1912).[38] Influenced by Phoebe Palmer, and appalled by a pamphlet "which denied the right of Mrs. Palmer and other women to preach,"[39] she wrote her own thirty-two page tract entitled *Female Ministry*. In it she laments the inequality of women as "a remarkable device of the devil," but she triumphantly proclaims, "the time of her deliverance draweth nigh." Indeed, Booth was "an unfailing, unflinching, uncompromising cham-

---

[35] Dayton and Dayton, 8-10; Deen, 237-245; Nancy Hardesty, *Great Women of Faith* (Grand Rapids: Baker, 1980), 103-109; Catherine Booth, *Aggressive Christianity* (Boston: The Christian Witness, 1899).

[36] Hardesty, 107.

[37] Hardesty, 104.

[38] Hardesty, 104.

[39] F. De L. Booth-Tucker, *The Life of Catherine Booth*, vol. 1 (New York: Fleming H. Revell, 1892), 348; Dayton and Dayton, 8.

pion of woman's rights."[40] As a result of her efforts, the Salvation Army has always ordained women and has tended to promote Biblical equality.

Mrs. Amanda Matthews-Berry Smith (1837-1915)[41] was born the child of slave parents in the State of Maryland. Inspired by Phoebe Palmer to fulfill her call to ministry, she began preaching in 1870 and encountered heartless racism and barbarous sexism. But Smith, despite having only three months of formal schooling, was both highly articulate and wonderfully anointed. Consequently, she gained remarkable respect from the educated and uneducated alike.[42] She ministered with great success throughout America, the British Isles, Liberia, Sierra Leone, Burma, and India where she was commended by Methodist Bishop Thoburn.[43]

---

[40] Booth-Tucker, 123.

[41] Amanda Smith, *An Autobiography: The Story of the Lord's Dealings with Mrs. Amanda Smith, the Colored Evangelist*; Hardesty, 117-122; Dean, 251-258.

[42] Dayton and Dayton, 15.

[43] Hardesty, 121.

WHAT WAS IT ABOUT PHOEBE THAT PROMPTED THE LORD TO POSE THE QUESTION, "WHERE ARE MY PHOEBES?"

Was it her obedient heart? Her willingness to pay the price? Was it her determination to keep Him first in her life? To order her life as He required? Was it her questioning mind? Her need to find answers? Her habit of asking Him for answers? Was it her habit of encouraging men and other women to become all that God wanted then to become? What was it?

"Where are My Phoebes?" the Lord asks.

Chapter 4

Where Are
My Aimees?

A IMEE SEMPLE MCPHERSON (1890-1944) was born in Ingersoll, Ontario, Canada. Her father, James Morgan Kennedy, was an organist in the Methodist church, and when Aimee was very young, he began teaching her to play the piano and the organ. Her mother, Mildred Pearce Kennedy, orphaned at twelve, was reared by the Salvation Army.

Aimee was seventeen when she was converted at a revival conducted by Robert James Semple, an itinerant Pentecostal evangelist. Semple, a native of Magherafelt, Northern Ireland, was a kindly and simple man, a boilermaker by trade. On August 12, 1908, Aimee and Robert married. They held meetings in various towns and pioneered a church in the Ontario town of Stratford before moving to Chicago in January, 1909. There they were ordained by

William Durham. For several months, they worked with him in evangelistic campaigns.

In 1910, the Semples went to China as faith missionaries. Arriving in June, they both fell ill almost immediately with malaria or typhoid fever. It was a tragic scene. Pregnant with her first child, Aimee recovered, but on August 19, 1910, Robert died. Aimee remained in Hong Kong until Roberta Star Semple was born a month later.

The tragedy intensified when Aimee and her newborn arrived in America. Instead of being embraced with compassion and concern by the Christian community, they were abandoned as failures!

It's hard to imagine how Aimee must have felt! Grief. Pain. Abandonment. Hopelessness. Fear. Confusion. Doubt. Barely twenty years old, and alone, distraught, and bewildered, she and her newborn infant retreated to her parents' home. Before long, she and her mother went to New York City and worked in a Salvation Army hostel.[1]

In New York, Aimee met Harold Stewart McPherson (1890-1968), a Providence, Rhode Island bookkeeper. Who can really know her motive for marriage at this time? It had been hardly more than a year since the tragic loss of dear Robert in

---

[1] Stanley E. Burgess and Gary B. McGee, eds., *Dictionary of Pentecostal and Charismatic Movements* (Grand Rapids: Zondervan, 1988), 568-569.

far-away China. Was she truly in love with McPherson? Or was she enamored by his charm and status? Or perhaps she was enticed by his promise of provision and earthly security. Regardless, Aimee and McPherson wed on February 28, 1912. Their son Rolf Kennedy McPherson was born on March 23, 1913.

Aimee had indeed found earthly security, but it had come at the expense of her relationship with God. Before long she fell severely ill and hovered between life and death. At this critical moment, she recommitted her life to the Lord. She vowed to trust Him unreservedly, to look to no one but Him to care for her, and to serve no one but Him only. Death lost its grip and her healing began.

Then one night in 1915, still recuperating, Aimee bundled up five-year-old Roberta and two-year-old Rolph, and slipped out of the house. Escaping, as it were, to her parents' home in Canada, she continued to recover. She also attended a Pentecostal campmeeting, and there she experienced full physical restoration and spiritual renewal.

Young Mr. McPherson loved Aimee and pursued her to Canada. They launched an evangelistic ministry together, conducting their first meeting in East Providence, R.I., in June, 1916. Then for two years, Aimee and company toured the Eastern seaboard in her *Gospel Auto* holding tent meetings from Washburn, Maine to Key West, Florida. In June 1917,

Aimee began writing and publishing her monthly magazine, *The Bridal Call.*

Evangelistic ministry is not glamorous, as some may suppose! The demands and hardships that accompany evangelistic ministry took their toll on the McPhersons, and Aimee faced tragedy of a new sort. The marriage collapsed completely and Harold returned to Providence. He filed for divorce, and it was granted in August, 1921.[2]

Aimee, accompanied by Roberta, Rolph, and her mother, "Minnie" Kennedy, pushed on. She did the only thing she knew to do, and that was to preach in obedience to the call of God. In the fall of 1918, the little band made a transcontinental *Gospel Tour,* ending in Los Angeles. There Aimee found favor and established her headquarters.

The subsequent years brought rapid expansion. Between 1918 and 1923, she and her mother crisscrossed America eight times. With great success, they conducted thirty-eight revivals in tents, churches, theaters, and auditoriums in Philadelphia, San Francisco, Baltimore, San Diego, Washington, D.C., Dayton, Denver, Montreal, Hartford, the Bronx, Indianapolis, St. Louis, and elsewhere. Aimee's Denver revivals (1921 and 1922) attracted no less than 12,000 people every night for a month,

---

[2] Burgess and McGee, 569.

and she enjoyed the support of prominent leaders including the mayor and the governor.

1922 was a watershed year for Aimee. In 1919, the Assemblies of God had ordained Aimee as an evangelist, but her divorce disqualified her from ordination with this denomination, so in January, 1922, she returned the papers.[3] It was also in 1922 that she began construction of her permanent ministry center, Angelus Temple in Los Angeles. The same year in San Francisco, she broadcast the first radio sermon in history delivered by a woman. 1922 was also the year she ministered in Australia.

The center in Los Angeles quickly grew into a significant, multifarious operation. On January 1, 1923, she dedicated the one million dollar, 5,300 seat Angelus Temple, and for three years she preached every night[4] and three times on Sundays to capacity crowds. Her dramatized sermons, robed choirs, orchestra, and brass band attracted wide attention. In 1924, she began operating her own 500-watt radio station, KFSG in Los Angeles, thus becoming the first woman to receive an FCC license to operate a radio station.[5] In 1927 she

[3] Burgess and McGee, 569.

[4] Edward T. James, ed., "McPherson, Aimee Semple." *Notable American Women 1607-1950. A Biographical Dictionary*, vol. 2 (Cambridge: Belknap Press, 1971), 477-480.

[5] Burgess and McGee, 570.

opened the Angelus Temple Commissary which was replenished each Sunday as the people brought food or clothing for distribution to the needy. She opened a prayer tower, where volunteers spent two-hour prayer shifts, twenty-four hours a day, and where counselors offered round-the-clock spiritual and practical help by telephone. Aimee mobilized soul-winning endeavors, instituted a free employment bureau and parole committee, and conducted summer camps and Bible conferences.[6] In addition to all of this, Aimee wrote and published her own works, including weekly and monthly periodicals.

She had begun calling her message the *Foursquare Gospel* in July 1922.[7] In 1927, she incorporated her ministry, calling it *the International Church of the Foursquare Gospel.*[8] The *foursquare* concept had come by way of revelation during a time of praise and worship during a revival in Oakland, California. An overflow congregation had crowded the great tent, and on the platform were pastors from Episcopal, Presbyterian, Baptist, Congregational, Methodist, Nazarene, Salvation Army, Christian and Missionary Alliance, and Pentecostal churches. Aimee recalls the revelation:

---

[6] James, 479.

[7] James, 478.

[8] Burgess and McGee, 570.

My soul was awed. The blazing glory of that heavenly vision seemed to fill and permeate not only the tabernacle, but the whole earth. In the clouds of heaven, Ezekiel had beheld that Being, whose glory no mortal can describe. As he gazed upon that marvelous revelation of the Omnipotent One, he perceived four faces. The faces—those of a man, a lion, an ox, and an eagle. These four faces likened unto the four phases of the Gospel of Jesus Christ.

In the face of the Man I saw the Man of sorrows, One acquainted with grief, dying on the tree.

In the face of the Lion I saw the mighty baptizer with the Holy Ghost and fire.

In the face of the Ox was typified the Great Burden-bearer, Who Himself took our infirmities and carried our sickness.

In the face of the Eagle I saw reflected the Coming King, our Bridegroom, Who would soon come to catch His beloved bride away.

It was a perfect Gospel. A complete Gospel for body, for soul, for spirit, and for eternity. A Gospel that faces squarely in every direction.

The whole tent was enveloped. It was as though every soul was brought into harmony with celestial music. I stood still there and listened, gripping the pulpit, shaking with wonder, then I exclaimed: "Why—why it's the

Foursquare Gospel!"[9]

In her *Foursquare* message, Aimee asserted that that humanity can be

released from the hold of sin, redeemed to be all he was originally intended to be, empowered to offensively permeate this planet with resurrection life, and infused with the hope of the immanent return of the King.[10]

In 1925, in response to the overwhelming demand to travel to all parts of the world to minister, Aimee opened Angelus Temple Training Institute. She would share the responsibility by training others to answer the call. The institute, located next to the Temple in the Lighthouse of International Foursquare Evangelism, soon became known as L.I.F.E. Bible College.

The purpose of the institute is two-fold: the preparation of Evangelists and Missionaries for the field; and a thorough Bible instruction for those not expecting to enter the field, but desiring knowledge of the Word of God. Its purpose is to fit men and women to be practi-

---

[9] Pamphlet: "Ministering Wholeness, Healing, Power, Hope." Los Angeles: Foursquare Publications, 1983.

[10] Pamphlet: "Ministering Wholeness, Healing, Power, Hope." Los Angeles: Foursquare Publications, 1983.

cal winners of souls, able to cope with the most difficult situations and to come out more than conquerors by the power of the Holy Spirit; to give a thorough understanding of the Foursquare Gospel and the knowledge of how to impart it to others.[11]

Aimee's flare for the dramatic was not absent for a moment at the dedication on January 1, 1926. It was a gala event indeed! She recalls,

The dedication of the great six and a half story new School Building was the event of the day. How eagerly everyone looked forward to this particular afternoon when God's blessing and His Spirit's presence would be invoked. The students and children of the Temple looked happiest of all, for this was specially to be their building. Here they would be free to study the "good news of God" and prepare to go not all the world with it. With banners showing where they came from— United States, Canada, England, Scotland, Australia, New Zealand, Europe,—they marched proudly to the door of the building. Had our Sister McPherson ever looked happier? Here was her dream materialized, the child of her fancy. . . . The Bible! The Bible! We love it,

---

[11] *L.I.F.E. Bible College Yearbook 1926*, 17.

we believe it, we want it in the hearts of the next generation![12]

A creative genius, Aimee's innovations facilitated the personal growth of her students and the corporate growth of her network of ministries. In *L.I.F.E* Bible College, she offered both Day and Night School. Students in the Day School participated in evangelistic outreaches in shops and factories, hospitals and jails, while Night School students invented other ways to channel their evangelistic zeal. Besides sharing her own experiences with the students, Aimee facilitated other "missionaries of years of experience on the battle front in various countries" who gave "practical talks on their joys and sorrows, and what we must expect in our future conquests for Jesus."[13]

Needless to say, the Bible school flourished. Its graduates lost no time in establishing home and foreign missionary outreaches. Branch churches sprang up first in the environs of Los Angeles; in fact, in no time, thirty-two churches had been established in southern California and fifty others were appealing to Angelus Temple for permission to affiliate.[14]

---

[12] *L.I.F.E. Bible College Yearbook 1926*, 20.

[13] *L.I.F.E. Bible College Yearbook* 1926, 61.

[14] John Thomas Nichol, *Pentecostalism* (New York: Harper & Rowe, 1966), 121.

At the time of Aimee's untimely death in 1944, L.I.F.E. Bible College had graduated over 3,000 ordained missionaries, evangelists, and pastors. Many of these were women. Her organization had over 400 branches in the United States and Canada, almost 200 mission stations abroad, and about 22,000 church members.[15]

The later 1920s and early 1930s were especially difficult years for Aimee. Critics sarcastically dubbed her the *Barnum of religion*, the *Mary Pickford of revivalism*, and the *titian-haired whoopee evangelist.*[16] In May, 1926, while swimming at a beach near Los Angeles, she mysteriously dropped out of sight. A month later, she surfaced in Mexico claiming she had been kidnapped. In legal proceedings that followed, she was indicted for conspiracy to obstruct justice and for perjury, but all charges against her were dropped because of lack of evidence.

Aimee's troubles did not stop there. In 1928, she had a bitter quarrel with her mother. In 1930, she had a nervous breakdown before entering an ill-fated marriage to David L. Hutton in 1931.[17] In 1936, she was estranged from her daughter.

But Aimee was a survivor. She continued to minister until her untimely death on September 26,

---

[15] James, 479.

[16] James, 479.

[17] James, 479.

1944. She died of an overdose of sleeping pills. She was buried in Forest Lawn Cemetery in Glendale, California, on October 9, 1944, in one of the largest funerals ever held in Los Angeles.[18] Thus ended the earthly life, but not the profound influence of a woman of God who has been hailed as "undoubtedly the most prominent woman leader Pentecostalism has produced to date."[19]

WHAT WAS IT ABOUT AIMEE THAT PROMPTED THE LORD TO POSE THE QUESTION, "WHERE ARE MY AIMEES?"

Was it her uninhibited style? Her acceptance of who she was? Her creative genius? Was it her flare for the dramatic, making her a dynamic communicator? Was it her commitment to Him? Her willingness to motivate and facilitate others for His service? Was it her love of people? Was it her willingness to spend her life in unselfish, Christ-centered, Spirit-empowered service to others, especially those in need. Was it her determination to go on trusting God in spite of tragedy and pain? What was it?

"Where are My Aimees?" the Lord asks.

---

[18] Burgess and McGee, 571.

[19] Burgess and McGee, 571.

Chapter 5

What Makes the Difference?

HY DID THE LORD ASK ME to consider Susanna, Phoebe, and Aimee? (God always has a purpose in communicating with us!)

Each woman was a vessel of honor empowered by the Holy Spirit for Divine service. Vessels of honor, yes. Perfect, no. The power of God that flowed through them was a gift of grace, freely bestowed, not a badge earned. It was a trust demanding responsible stewardship.

Susanna, Phoebe, Aimee—at some point while still young, each responded wholeheartedly to God's call. This provided a purpose that reached beyond the dictates of culture and religion. It removed many restrictions of earth-bound living by instilling a sense of eternal values. It instilled a reason for being ordained by God. It gave the awareness of being more than a womb and more than a worker. It preempted expectations of friend and foe alike, requiring instead full cooperation with God.

There was no room for compromise. Each woman's resources were fully yielded to the call. Her time, her talents, her energy, her relationships—all were surrendered to God. Motherhood for Susanna served as a classroom equipping both her and her children to fulfil divine destiny. Phoebe, on the other hand, had to surrender her cherished offspring to the care of others.

Preparation to fulfill the divine mandate, in fact, came in many forms. Sometimes it meant overcoming crushing difficulties, tragedy, and unimaginable pain. Lesser persons would have quit! But these women turned to God, trusting Him for protection, provision, and power. As a result, they, like Jesus, came out of the wilderness with no confidence in natural strength or strategy, but wholly dependent on the Spirit. In turn, He could depend on them!

Preparation meant learning to lean on God when confronted with the incessant, demoralizing, ugly face of sexism. But each of these women knew her true identity was not resident in her gender; it was found in her relationship with her Savior, Jesus Christ. Furthermore, each one knew her call was not from men or institutions, but directly from God the Creator, the Almighty One.

What role did education play in their lives? Since these women lived in times when education was reserved either primarily or exclusively for boys and men, none was the recipient of formal theological education. They did not use this injustice as an excuse for ignorance. Rather, each prized knowledge and found ways to learn and grow. Susanna learned languages today reserved for seminary graduates. Phoebe was an avid student and prolific writer. Both entered theological debate well-prepared and confident.

Each of these three women experienced personal loss and tragedy, but none held God responsible. Instead, each one examined herself before God to see how she might make adjustments to become more conformed to His image. Susanna, alone and impoverished with many mouths to feed, emerged victorious as a mother and minister in a church hostile to women in leadership. Phoebe, devastated by the deaths of her beloved babies, repented of idolatry and became the woman God wanted her to be. Aimee had so many opportunities to turn away from the church and from God! She could have been completely destroyed and rendered useless by the death of her devoted, missionary husband in China. She could have become embittered and callous when the Pentecostal Christians rejected her as a failure when she returned from China, a widow at twenty with a newborn and nowhere to go. Where were church people when she needed them most? They were not there. But God was, and she began to learn that He would never leave her, that he would never forsake her.

Perhaps we should consider the effect of the marriage relationship in these women's lives. Susanna and Phoebe enjoyed the respect and full support of their spouses. Phoebe, in particular, was blessed in this regard. I have often wondered how Aimee's life would have been different had she had such sacrificial support. Would she still have had a nervous breakdown? Would she still have died of an overdose of sleeping pills? What if Robert Semple had lived? What if Harold McPherson and David Hutton had been willing to serve selflessly in the shadows? What if they, like Dr. Walter Palmer, had been willing to look after the home while his wife studied, prayed, and traveled? What if they, like him, had been willing to start a publishing company to extend her influence? What if they, like him, had been willing to leave the prestige of the medical profession to carry his wife's suitcases while she received the attention and acclaim? What a difference it might have made!

Susanna, Phoebe, and Aimee—they still have much to say to us all. Susanna was a torch for truth in the eighteenth century; Phoebe, in the nineteenth century; and Aimee, in the twentieth century. Who will it be in the twenty-first century? Who will it be in your day? Will it be you?

Chapter 6

Will You Answer the Call?

By Barbara Silver

W ILL YOU ANSWER THE CALL OF GOD? Will you answer the call to be one of His appointed and anointed Women of God? Will you respond to that call and receive the anointing according to Joel 2:28-29 and Acts 2:17-18?

And it shall come to pass in the last days, says God, That I will pour out of My Spirit on all flesh; Your sons and your daughters shall prophesy. Your young men shall see visions. Your old men shall dream dreams. And on My menservants and on My maidservants I will pour out My Spirit in those days; And they shall prophesy (Acts 2:17-18 NKJV).

You can receive the high calling of God to walk in His ways and to fulfill His divine plan and unique purpose for your life. Submit to Him; let God develop His gifts within you. You are called to do Kingdom business, to be about your Father's work. You were created and ordained to do good works!

For we are God's workmanship, created in Christ Jesus to do good works, which God prepared in advance for us to do (Eph. 2:10 NIV).

Answer God's call to fulfill His purpose in your life. Respond to the leading of the Holy Spirit and submit to the anointings which He has placed on your life. He has need of you! He has a specific plan and purpose for you. That purpose is ordained by God. Become a vessel of honor, empowered by His grace, His supernatural ability to do all that you need to do and all that He asks you to do. God will *make all grace abound to you, so that in all things at all times, having all that you need, you will abound in every good work (2 Cor. 9:8 NIV).*

Receive His grace now. Receive God's supernatural ability so that you may be anointed and empowered by His Spirit for Divine service.

TO RESPOND TO THE CALL, WHETHER FOR THE FIRST TIME OR AS A RECOMMITMENT, PRAY THIS PRAYER:

Father God, fill me with your grace, your supernatural ability to do all that I'm called to do. Let your unconditional love and compassion fill me and flow through me to others.

Father, I submit my life to you. I receive the call and I ask that you anoint me. Fulfill your divine plan and purpose in me. Create the vision within me. Holy Spirit, teach me and fill me. Jesus, be Lord over my life.

Let your victory and knowledge of the truth that set me free be revealed through me to set others free.

Now Father, heal me of the hurts of the past that would hinder me from submitting my life to you. Heal me of all the opposition that has come against me and all the effects of that opposition to my purpose. Heal me of the memories of those hurts. And Father, I ask that you give me the **miracle** to walk as if they never happened, in Jesus' Name. Cleanse the old images that are not in line with God's will for my life and give me the new image of walking hand-in-hand with God, being submitted to Him, fulfilling His plan and purpose for my life, being empowered by grace and filled with love, walking in authority over the enemy and being that vessel of honor, called and ordained by God.

According to Mark 11:22-25, we are to speak to our mountains. So I speak to all opposition coming against me and tell it to bow the knee and go, in Jesus' Name. I ask God to fill every place, to be my Provider, Protector, and Shield, and give me direction and clarity of purpose, in Jesus' Name. I take authority over opposition rising up again. It is bound in Jesus' name (Mt. 16:19).

I ask God to give me the boldness to speak, teach, and minister as a woman of God—called, appointed, and anointed. I want to walk as Jesus walked (1 Jn. 2:6) and say only what I hear the father say and do only what I see the Father do, for it's the Father in me doing His work (Jn.

Where Are My Susannas?

8:26, 28; 12:49-50; 5:19; 14:10). I can do nothing of my-
self, but through Christ, I can do all things (Jn. 5:19, 30;
8:28; Phil. 4:13).

Father, I submit my life to you,
Not my will but thine to do.
Circumcise my heart, I pray;
Make me clean and pure to stay.
Let me walk in all your ways,
Serving you throughout my days.
Let me hear your voice today;
Spirit of Truth, teach me your way.
In Jesus' name, Amen.

As you submit to God, you will see God unfold
His master plan for your life. Let this prayer and
these confessions become real to you. Watch God
use you as He daily leads and guides you into your
Divine purpose.

God **will** pour out His Spirit on you and you
will prophesy. He will reveal truth to you. As that
revelation knowledge is freely given to you, you will
freely give it to others, so that the truth will set the
captives free (Mt. 10:8; Jn. 8:32). Hold back no
longer! God has need of you. He desires to use you
to perfect the saints and bring His body into unity
in the faith (Eph. 4:12, 13). His grace is sufficient
for all your needs, for all that you need in your
ministry and in your personal life. You are anointed
to walk as Jesus walked.

The Spirit of the Lord is on me, because he has anointed me to preach good news to the poor. He has sent me to proclaim freedom for the prisoners and recovery of sight for the blind, to release the oppressed, to proclaim the year of the Lord's favor (Lk. 4:18-19 NIV).

Just as the Spirit anointed Jesus, He will anoint you. The Holy Spirit will anoint you to flow in all five functions of the ministry (Eph. 4:11). He will anoint you—

- as an APOSTLE, *a sent one with a message,* to break through, to plow the ground, and to take authority over the enemy.

- as a PROPHET to decree and declare the Word of the Lord and to plant the seed, the Word of God, in the hearts of the people.

- as an EVANGELIST to draw all people into Jesus for their next step in Jesus, to proclaim the Good News, and to bring forth a harvest.

- as a PASTOR AND TEACHER to nourish, maintain, and feed the flock in order that they mature, multiply, and flourish.

Confession and Prayer

Father, I ask that you reveal all of these functions to me, according to the purpose and plan of my life. Give me wisdom, knowledge, understanding, discernment, revelation, and interpretation. Let me teach, preach, and heal the sick, just as Jesus did. Let your gifts flow through me as your Spirit wills (1 Cor. 12:11). I thank you, Father, that great signs, wonders, and miracles will follow me as I walk in your love and compassion. In Jesus' Name, Amen.

Making Your Calling Sure

You are fully equipped to fulfill His divine plan and ordained purpose for your life. Study these scriptures and let faith rise in your heart until you become fully persuaded that God is able to do through you what He promised in His word (Rm. 4:21).

2 Peter 1:3-8, 10(NIV)

[3]His divine power has given to us everything we need for life and godliness through our knowledge of him who called us by glory and goodness. [4]Through these he has given us his very great and precious promises, so that through them you may participate in the divine nature and escape the corruption in the world caused by evil desires. [5]For this very reason, make every effort to add to your faith goodness; and to goodness, knowledge; [6]and to knowledge, self-control; and to self-control, perseverance; and to perseverance, godliness; [7]and to godliness, brotherly kindness; and to brotherly kindness, love. [8]For if you possess these qualities in increasing measure, they will keep you from being ineffective and unproductive in your knowledge of our Lord Jesus Christ. [10]Therefore, my brothers, be all the more eager to make your calling and election sure. For if you do these things, you will never fall.

Colossians 3:12, 14, 16a, 17^(NIV)

¹²Therefore, as God's chosen people, holy and dearly loved, clothe yourselves with compassion, kindness, humility, gentleness and patience. ¹⁴And over all these virtues put on love, which binds them all together in perfect unity. ¹⁶Let the word of Christ dwell in you richly as you teach and admonish one antoher with all wisdom . . . ¹⁷And whatever you do, whether in word or deed, do it all in the name of the Lord Jesus, giving thanks to God the Father through him.

Ephesians 2:10^(NIV)

For we are God's workmanship, created in Christ Jesus for good works, which God prepared in advance for us to do.

2 Thessalonians 2:16a, 17^(NIV)

¹⁶ᵃMay our Lord Jesus Christ himself and God our Father . . . encourage your hearts and strengthen you in every good deed and word.

2 Timothy 2:20-21 ^(NIV)

²⁰In a large house there are articles not only of gold and silver, but also of wood and clay; some are for noble purposes and some for ignoble. ²¹If a man cleanses himself from the latter, he will be an instrument for noble purposes, made holy, useful to the Master and prepared to do any good work.

Ephesians 1:17-23^(NIV)

¹⁷I keep asking that the God of our Lord Jesus Christ, the glorious Father, so that you may know him better. [18]I pray that the eyes of your heart may be enlightened in order that you may know the hope to which he has called you, the riches of his glorious inheritance in the saints, [19]and his incomparably great power for us to believe. That power is like the working of his mighty strength, [20]which he exerted in Christ when he raised him from the dead and seated him at his right hand in the heavenly realms, [21]far above all rule and authority, power and dominion, and every title that can be given, not only in the present age but also in the one to come. [22]And God placed all things under his feet and appointed him to be head over everything in the church, [23]which is his body, the fullness of him who fills everything in every way.

Ephesians 3:16-21[(NIV)]

I pray that out of his glorious riches he may strengthen you with power through his Spirit in your inner being, [17]so that Christ may dwell in your hearts through faith. And I pray that you, being rooted and established in love, [18]may have power, together with all the saints, to grasp how wide and long and high and deep is the love of Christ, [19]and to know this love that surpasses knowledge—that you may be filled to the measure of all the fullness of God. [20]Now to him who is able to do immeasurably more than all we ask or imagine, according to his power that is at work within us, [21]to him be glory in the church and in Christ Jesus throughout all generations, for ever and ever! Amen.

Isaiah 11:2^(NIV)

The Spirit of the LORD will rest on him—the Spirit of wisdom and of understanding, the Spirit of counsel and of power, the Spirit of knowledge and of the fear of the LORD.

Colossians 1:9-12^(NIV)

⁹We have not stopped praying for you and asking God to fill you with the knowledge of his will through all spiritual wisdom and understanding. ¹⁰And we pray this in order that you may live a life worthy of the Lord and may please him in every way; bearing fruit in every good work, growing in the knowledge of God, ¹¹being strengthened with all power according to his glorious might so that you may have great endurance and patience, and joyfully ¹²giving thanks to the Father, who has qualified you to share in the inheritance of the saints in the kingdom of light.

1 Timothy 6:11-12^(NIV)

¹¹ . . . pursue righteousness, godliness, faith, love, endurance and gentleness. ¹²Fight the good fight of faith. Take hold of the eternal life to which you were called. . . .

Philippians 1:9-11^(NIV)

⁹And this I pray: that your love may abound more and more in knowledge and depth of insight, 10so that you may be able to discern what is best and may be pure and blameless until the day of Christ, 11filled with the fruit of righteousness that comes through Jesus Christ—to the glory and praise of God.

Where Are My Susannas?

1 Thessalonians 5:16-18*(NIV)*

[16]*Be joyful always;* [17]*pray continually;* [18]*give thanks in all circumstances, for this is God's will for you in Christ Jesus.*

2 Timothy 2:22, 24-25*(NIV)*

[22]*. . . pursue righteousness, faith, love and peace . . .* [24]*And the Lord's servant must not quarrel; instead, he must be kind to everyone, able to teach, not resentful.* [25]*Those who oppose him he must gently instruct, in the hope that God will grant them repentance leading them to a knowledge of the truth.*

Jeremiah 29:11-13*(NIV)*

[11]*For I know the plans I have for you," declares the LORD, "plans to prosper you and not to harm you, plans to give you hope and a future.* [12]*Then you will call upon me and come and pray to me, and I will listen to you.* [13]*You will seek me and find me when you seek me with all your heart.*

A Gift for You

A few years ago, God asked my husband, Sam, to fast. God instructed him to fast a total of 270 days over a span of time. When he had completed the fast, God told him that this 270-day period of fasting, equal to a 9-month period, was like a birthing period for a Move of God. This fast was to be given to the body of Christ and applied to their account in heaven. They could draw on that account **by faith** at will.

During this time, God had him study and receive by faith the benefits of a fast, according to Isaiah 58:6-14(NIV). These benefits are as follows:

> *v. 6 "Is not this the kind of fasting that I have chosen: to loose the chains of injustice and untie the cords of the yoke, to set the oppressed free and break every yoke?*
>
> *v. 8 Then your light will break forth like the dawn, and your healing will quickly appear; then your righteousness will go before you, and the glory of the Lord will be your rear guard.*
>
> *v. 9a Then you will call, and the Lord will answer; you will cry for help, and he will say: Here am I.*
>
> *v. 10b Then your light will rise in the darkness, and your night will become like the noonday.*
>
> *v. 11 The Lord will guide you always; he will satisfy your needs in a sun-scorched land and will strengthen your frame. You will be like a well-watered garden, like a spring whose waters never fail.*
>
> *v. 12b You will be called Repairer of Broken Walls, Restorer of Streets with Dwellings.*
>
> *v. 14 Then you will find your joy in the Lord, and I will cause you to ride on the heights of the land and to feast on the inheritance of your father Jacob."*
>
> *The mouth of the Lord has spoken.*

Then after the fasting was finished, God told him to extend the benefits of the fast to others and to tell them to receive these benefits by faith in the Word of God. God instructed him to tell people to receive the benefits as a gift from Jesus to them, as if they had done the fasting themselves. They should appropriate the benefits not only for themselves, their families and those for whom they were called to pray, but also to use the benefits in ministering to others. Many times there are strongholds in our lives and others' lives that need to be broken. The promises in God's Word concerning fasting will break these yokes of bondage or chains of injustice, so that we can be free to serve God to the fullness of our purpose.

So receive by faith these benefits of the fast. When you cry out to God, He says, *"Here am I"* (Is. 58:9 NIV), and when the **Great I Am** is on the scene, you have all that you need. The fasting has been done and you can be set free. Jesus said, *"This kind can come out by nothing but prayer and fasting"* (Mk. 9:29 NKJV). So if there is bondage or a yoke that needs to be broken, receive it broken by faith. God's grace is sufficient and your healings will quickly appear. Jesus paid the price so that you would not have to. He loves you so much.

Then as you minister to others, pray that the benefits of the fast be applied to them, so they will be free from bondage and able to submit to God. This is a gift from God. Freely you have been given and now freely you can give (Mt. 10:8).

A Note about Rev. Barbara T. Silver

In 1978 Barbara Silver was miraculously healed of an incurable disease. Knowing nothing about divine healing at the time, she trusted that God in His unconditional love for her would not let her die. After the healing of her physical body, God continued to minister His healing for her emotions from the hurts and effects of the battles and struggles of life.

Soon, Barbara felt the call to ministry. Together, she and her husband, J. Samuel Silver, founded Love Covenant Ministries. Barbara has been taking the messages of healing hurts, Biblical equality, God's unconditional love, authority over the devil, and the principles for abundant living to people around the country. As God pours out His revelation to her, she shares with others. Their ministry emphasizes the application of God's Word and wisdom in every aspect of life.

Presently, Barbara and Sam co-pastor Victory Christian Center of Atlanta. They have one daughter, Kimberly, who is attending Oral Roberts University. Along with their responsibilities as parents and pastors, they continue to travel and minister around the United States.

Barbara would be delighted to hear from you.

Rev. Barabara T. Silver
P. O. Box 451188
Atlanta, GA 31145

Phone (770) 270-0320   Fax (770) 270-0284

A Note about Susan Hyatt

Susan Hyatt is a seasoned minister and professional educator. Her passion is to see genuine Christianity prevail over fallen culture and human-centered religion. Within genuine Biblical Christianity, she believes, is everything that will enable believers to flourish in every aspect of life.

Susan is a Bible scholar and Pentecostal/Charismatic historian. She graduated with honors from University of New Brunswick Teachers' College and Christ for the Nations Institute, and *magna cum laude* from Southwestern Assemblies of God College. She earned M.A.s *with honors* from Oral Roberts University in Pentecostal/Charismatic Studies and Biblical Literature. She is pursuing Ph.D. studies at Fuller Theological Seminary.

Susan and her husband Eddie L. Hyatt are partners in life and ministry. Together they have planted and pastored churches, founded Bible schools, ministered internationally, and produced teaching material. They are co-founders of Hyatt Int'l Ministries, a vehicle that facilitates the teaching and equipping of God's people for End-Time revival.

Susan's new book, *Let's Keep the River Flowing,* is expected to be available in the summer of 1997. To purchase a copy or to receive information about other materials from Hyatt Int'l Ministries, contact:

Hyatt Int'l Ministries
P. O. Box 700276
Tulsa, OK 74170

Phone/Fax (918) 494-5763   E-Mail SHyatt3641@aol.com